Shaped Pasta

Cooking with Whimsy

Recipes & Far Fetched Food Fables from the Cooks at

◆ **Buckeye Beans** ◆

Our thanks

to Buckeye's staff and crew,

who tasted and tested

these recipes for you.

Copyright© 1996 Buckeye Beans & Herbs, Inc.
P.O. Box 28201
Spokane, Washington 99228-8201
1-800-227-1686

Library of Congress Catalogue Number: 96-084568

ISBN: 0-9652278-0-4

Edited, Designed, and Manufactured by:
Favorite Recipes® Press
P.O. Box 305142
Nashville, Tennessee 37230
1-800-358-0560

Copywriting/Text: Laura Mathisen/Jill Smith
Recipe Development: Jill Smith/Carol Dingwall
Cover Photography and Design: Robert Johnson
Project Manager: Bonita Zahara
Project Assistants: Kirsten Melgard, Dori Hettinger, Barbara Eliason

Manufactured in the United States of America
First Printing: 1996 75,000 copies

Recipe for cover photo, Holiday Magic Salad, is on page 51.
Recipes for back cover photographs, Hearty Minestrone Soup
and Perfect-Pitch Primavera, are on pages 18 and 34.

Dedication

This cookbook is dedicated to "making people smile."

Jill Smith
"Bean Queen"

Preface

Why a Cookbook on Shaped Pasta?

This is not just another pasta cookbook. But then shaped pasta is not just any old pasta. Shaped pasta is a new art form in food production that's creating a boiling hot revolution in modern eating. Buckeye Beans, an innovator and leader in the shaped pasta market, is constantly asked, "How do I use these funny shapes?" Most people know pasta begins with boiling water. But what to do with bunnies and baseballs?

The answer is "have some fun!" Shaped pasta *is* cooking with whimsy. It brings fun to the table and interest to traditional pasta meals. But it's not spaghetti! And although traditional spaghetti recipes work with shaped pasta, not all shaped-pasta recipes will work with spaghetti. That's why Buckeye compiled this book. It's a collection of easy and unusual recipes that take the guesswork out of cooking with whimsical shaped pasta.

How Shaped Pasta Came Into Being . . . The Technology of Shaped Pasta

Shaped pasta is a relatively new food product, made possible thanks to advances in modern production technology. Like its predecessor macaroni, shaped pasta requires a special coarse grind of flour known as semolina. The texture of semolina helps pasta take "shape" and maintain molecular structure through what is called the "extrusion technique" of pasta production. Extrusion, meaning "forced through," is a traditional method of producing pasta in which flour and water are blended, then forced under high pressure through a "die," a large steel disc that contains many small, intricately cut holes that form the shape. Wet pasta dough is forced through the top of the die, while on the bottom of the die a cutter spins to cut off the shapes. New technology allows die makers to design detailed pasta forms, with the ability to calculate pasta wall dimensions. The integrity of the pasta wall is all important in creating shaped pasta. If the wall of the shape is too thin, the pasta will fall apart in water; if too thick, the shapes twist and distort while cooking.

Contents

Fables

Standing Together in Green

◆

ong ago, the coniferous forest had no color. Choosing a color was no easy task. For the trees soon discovered they could not agree, and opinion splintered. At first, the Firs proposed yellow, but the Yews said that was a sappy color. The Spruces suggested blue. But the Cedars and Sequoias demanded red. To that, the Junipers responded they would, 'rather be deadwood than redwood,' which angered the Hemlocks, who said that 'could be arranged.' Listening to all of this, the Cypresses began to weep, while the shrubs decided to just lay low.

hey needled each other, until soon no tree would bend to the others' points of view. Just when all seemed hopeless, a Pine whispered a noble idea on the wind. 'We survive thanks to the bold yellow sun and nourishing blue water. Together, these colors would make us green.' It seemed so natural! So the trees agreed to stand together and be green. Soon everyone envied the forest's color and wanted to be green . . . first the grass, then the frogs, and today, even the politicians!

e honor the wisdom of that noble Pine, with the hope that our world will remain 'evergreen.'

Introduction

What Your Mother Never Told You About Playing With Your Food . . .

So your mother told you never to play with your food. Although you should always listen to your mother, times have changed. Shaped pasta is a new food form "cut out" just for play.

Featuring the things that smiles are made of, these pages let you discover soups, salads, sautés, and celebrations as playful as shaped pasta itself. From creative recipes to family-friendly craft ideas, this recipe book for dry shaped pasta is anything but dry. It's full of healthful and unusual recipes that challenge the tradition of red or white sauce on pasta.

With easy instructions and variations, this book invites you to experiment with the recipes. Go ahead and change the ingredients, try different pasta shapes, mix textures . . . play with the food!

The idea is to have as much fun in the kitchen as you have eating the results. And if these simple and creative recipes don't bring a smile to your face, we've added a few far fetched food fables that will.

The purpose of Shaped Pasta is to offer playful ways to bring whimsy to good eating. So, forget what mom said and have some fun. You've got our permission to play with your food. Enjoy!

Welcome to the World of Shaped Pasta

It's a topsy-turvy world of new pasta-bilities. Forget the admonishment to not play with your food. Why settle for the old straight and narrow noodle when you can have fun playing with your pasta shapes? Welcome to trees, leaves, sportsballs, and bicycles that add fun and fancy to your favorite pasta recipe. And forget worrying that if it's good and filling it must be bad for you. For health-conscious eating made simple, high-fat white and red sauces are being replaced by variations that cut the fat.

Cooking with Whimsy is more than just a collection of recipes; it is a guide to celebrating with family-friendly fun food. You'll find cooking instructions and creative ideas that invite families to both cook together and eat together. Remember when families sat around the table to enjoy a meal and tell stories of the day? In this fast-paced world, family storytelling has almost been forgotten. Many families don't have a chance to eat together, much less tell tales. So to bring a flavor to dinner, to spice up the pasta, we've added a few far fetched fables to the cookbook.

It doesn't take a lot to make a meal delightful, and our pastas are a celebration in fun, healthful eating. Attractive to display, with color appeal, they are kid friendly—easier than long noodles for little hands to manipulate, and fun to eat. And when food is fun, kids eat up.

Few things are as universal as pasta. The endless variety of shapes, sizes, textures, and colors allows pasta to adapt easily to any cuisine. Change the basic sauce ingredients, and you change the cuisine. To create simple pasta sauces with an international flair, add oriental sesame sauce for Chinese cuisine, rice vinegar or saki for Japanese, balsamic vinegar for Italian or Mediterranean, wine or crème fraîche for French, or salsa for American style. Create ten-minute pasta dishes by adding any mix and match of your own creation, such as flavored oils, cheeses, vegetables, nuts, or sauces.

PASTA BASICS

Nothing's more apt to
"make people smile,"
than a flavorful feast,
served up with style!

In the time that it takes
to cook pasta that's ordinary,
shaped pasta becomes a meal
that's extraordinary!
(and that's as basic as it gets!)

PASTA BASICS

How to Boil Water

If you can boil water, you can cook shaped pasta. To refine your water boiling technique, here are a few simple tips:

◆ Use a large enough pot so there is room to stir, and enough space above the waterline to prevent boiling over.

◆ Silly as it sounds, start with fresh cold water (cold because warm softened water can add unwanted salt).

◆ Turn on the heat. We suggest medium-high, to prevent scorching of pans. Bring water to a full boil before adding pasta. Now add salt if desired.

◆ Pour shaped pasta into rapidly boiling water, and immediately stir to the bottom of pan (to prevent sticking). Stir gently every two to three minutes until pasta is done.

◆ Draining techniques. When the pasta is done, pour through a colander in sink, add about a half inch of cold water to the bottom of the pot. Return to the warm, but off, stove burner. Place the colander in the top of the pot. Cover with a lid. The water steams the pasta in the colander to keep it hot until ready to serve.

◆ Modern draining techniques. Use a pasta pot with self-draining insert. Remove insert when ready, pour out water, add back a small amount of fresh water, place back on warm burner. Then return insert (full of pasta) to pot, cover until ready to serve. (We recommend the use of fresh water for steaming so the starch in the pasta cooking water will not stick to the bottom of the pot.)

Simple Cooking Tips to Guarantee Great Results
Perfect Pasta "Al Dente"

The Italians have an expression for properly cooked pasta. They call it 'al dente.' More than just the taste of the pasta or the way it's cooked, it's the experience of the texture in your mouth and on the palate. The literal translation of al dente is "to the tooth," meaning tender to the bite, not crunchy but still firm. Shaped pasta 'al dente' requires only that you drop the pasta in plenty of rapidly boiling water, stir occasionally and cook for seven to ten minutes, depending on the shape or size of the pasta. When the pasta is tender to the tooth, drain it quickly. It's that simple.

A few others (very few) believe that the term 'al dente' isn't even Italian. It actually began with a Chinese man named Ah Li, who worked in an Italian restaurant in New York. He spoke neither English nor Italian. His job was to cook the pasta. The chef instructed him to keep testing the pasta until he could 'dent' the noodles easily when he bit into them. "When you dentee, you callee," the chef said. So Ah Li tested the noodles this way and when they were just right (he had a natural noodle knack), he would cry "Ah Li dentee! Ah Li dentee!" And the name stuck (but of course the noodles didn't).

The Right Sauce

◆ Shaped pasta is a great alternative to traditional pasta in any and all recipes. As you get to know different shapes, you'll find some work better than others depending on the recipe. We suggest that you experiment with different shapes to find the best shape to enhance your eating experience.

◆ Salads—Generally, smaller shapes work better in salads than larger shapes, as they hold together better when tossing.

◆ Soups—Try more open shapes, as their lesser density complements the consistency of a light soup broth.

◆ Heavy Sauces—Larger shapes work well with heavy sauces, inviting the sauce to work its way into the grooves of the shape.

◆ Lighter Sauces—All pasta shapes work well with oil-based sauces.

◆ Family Meals—For small kids, who tend to like their pasta plain, use only a dash of sauce or none at all. Shaped pasta is perfect for little hands, as the shapes are easy to keep on a spoon or pick up.

How Much Pasta is Enough?

◆ Two ounces of dry shaped pasta makes about one cup cooked pasta, generally accepted as one serving.

◆ Shaped pasta will approximately double in volume with cooking.

Avoid Sticking

◆ Use a big pot, with enough space above the waterline to prevent boiling over.

◆ Use enough water so the pasta can easily move around as it boils.

◆ Optional. Add a splash of oil (we recommend olive oil) to the water before adding the pasta. A tablespoon will do for four to eight servings.

To Salt or Not To Salt

◆ Ask ten cooks why they salt pasta water and you'll get ten different answers.

◆ We believe salt in the cooking water enhances the flavor of pasta, and prevents the need to add salt at the table.

◆ Salt is optional in the cooking water.

Baking Pasta

◆ If the pasta is to be used in a baked casserole, shorten the boiling time by a few minutes to allow for additional cooking in the oven.

11

PASTA BASICS

Cooking Time

- Cooking time will vary with the pasta's size and shape.
- Always check the cooking time specified in the recipe or on the manufacturer's package.
- When in doubt, it's better to undercook than to overcook shaped pasta.
- Sample pasta near the end of the cooking time to test for doneness. Slightly chewy is perfect al dente. If it is slightly crunchy, it needs a little more time.

Serving Pasta Hot

- To avoid sticking, toss on a little oil or butter before adding the sauce.
- Pasta that is to be served immediately should not be rinsed or allowed to sit too long. To keep the pasta from cooling as it's served, heat the serving platter by immersing in hot water or warming in an oven.
- Tossing the pasta in the sauce works well, helping flavor the pasta consistently and preventing the pasta from sticking together. Drain, toss in enough sauce to coat and moisten, then serve. Try to avoid a puddle of sauce in the bottom of the bowl or platter.
- For very thick or chunky sauces, you may want to simply spoon the sauce on top of the pasta.

Pasta In Salads

- Pasta to be used in salads requires cooling before mixing into salad.
- To cool, simply rinse cooked pasta in cool water for a few minutes to lower the temperature of the pasta.
- Cooling the pasta helps maintain the integrity of the pasta shape when tossed with other salad ingredients.

Storing Cooked Pasta

- Lots of people love cold, leftover pasta.
- After cooking, rinse pasta to be stored with cold water.
- To store, add a dash of oil (to avoid sticking) and refrigerate in an airtight container.
- Freezing cooked pasta is not a good idea, unless, of course, you like mounds of pasta mush.
- Refrigerating cooked pasta in sauce works, but be aware that the pasta will continue to grow and absorb the sauce while in the refrigerator. (At Buckeye we call this the attack of the monster pasta bunnies!)

Trees and Cheese

A Favorite Recipe: *A new "twig" on an old favorite. This rich and creamy macaroni and cheese is a "spruced" up version of a timeless classic.*

◆

Pick-a-Pasta: This entrée stands tall using tree-shaped pasta.

◆

¹/₄	cup butter
¹/₄	cup flour
4	cups milk, heated
1	teaspoon prepared mustard
1	teaspoon salt, or to taste
¹/₈	teaspoon red pepper
2	teaspoons Worcestershire sauce
15	ounces shaped pasta, cooked, drained
4 to 5	cups shredded Cheddar cheese

Melt the butter in a saucepan. Stir in the flour until blended. Add the milk gradually, stirring constantly. Bring to a boil; reduce heat. Cook until thickened, stirring constantly. Stir in the mustard, salt, red pepper and Worcestershire sauce. Add the pasta and cheese and mix well. Cook until the cheese melts, stirring frequently, and serve. Baked version: Spoon the mixture into baking dish, sprinkle with additional cheese and/or buttered bread crumbs and bake at 350 degrees for 30 minutes. As a variation, add 2 cups steamed vegetables, 2 cups chopped smoked ham, 8 ounces crumbled crisp-fried bacon, 1 can drained tuna or sautéed onion and green bell pepper to the mixture.

Makes 6 servings

Approx Per Serving: Cal 828; Prot 39 g; Carbo 66 g; T Fat 46 g;
49% Calories from Fat; Chol 142 mg; Fiber 2 g; Sod 1131 mg

Toodle Nuna Casserole

Another Favorite Recipe: An easy-to-make tuna casserole with oceans of flavor.

◆

ℝick-a-ℝasta: Dolphin-shaped pasta plays well with the toodles in this nuna casserole.

◆

1	cup chopped onion
1	cup chopped celery
2	tablespoons butter
2	(6-ounce) cans tuna, drained
1	(15-ounce) can peas, drained
1	(10-ounce) can cream of mushroom soup
3/4	cup milk
1/2	cup sour cream
1/2	teaspoon salt
1/2	teaspoon pepper
6	ounces shaped pasta, cooked, drained
1	(3-ounce) can French-fried onions

Sauté the onion and celery in the butter in a skillet until tender. Combine the tuna, peas, soup, milk, sour cream, salt and pepper in a bowl and mix well. Fold in the onion mixture and pasta. Spoon into a buttered baking dish. Sprinkle with the French-fried onions. Bake at 350 degrees for 35 minutes. Serve with a green salad.

Makes 6 servings

Approx Per Serving: Cal 466; Prot 25 g; Carbo 45 g; T Fat 21 g;
40% Calories from Fat; Chol 41 mg; Fiber 4 g; Sod 1113 mg

Delicious Apple Salad

And Another Favorite Recipe: Shift into high gear with this new spin on a traditional Waldorf salad. A sweet, tart, and tantalizing cross-country classic.

◆

Pick-a-Pasta: Bicycle-shaped pasta is a must in this racy salad.

◆

2 cups uncooked shaped pasta
2 cups chopped red apples
1 cup chopped celery
1/2 cup walnut pieces
1 cup mayonnaise
2 tablespoons lemon juice
1 teaspoon sugar

Bring enough cold water to cover the pasta to a boil in a saucepan over medium-high heat. Add the pasta. Cook until al dente, stirring occasionally. Drain and rinse with cold water until cool. Combine the pasta, apples, celery and walnuts in a bowl and mix gently. Fold in a mixture of the mayonnaise, lemon juice and sugar. Chill, covered, until serving time. May add 1 cup whole cooked cranberries for a tangy flavor or 1/2 cup raisins or blueberries. May substitute any variety of apple for the red apples. May substitute almonds for the walnuts. Lower the fat grams by substituting a mixture of 1/2 cup mayonnaise and 1/2 cup nonfat yogurt for the mayonnaise.

Makes 6 servings

Approx Per Serving: Cal 489; Prot 7 g; Carbo 37 g; T Fat 36 g;
65% Calories from Fat; Chol 22 mg; Fiber 2 g; Sod 230 mg .

Vain Wayne of the Weather Vane

◆

Have you ever wondered why Roosters top weather vanes? It started, the Buckeye Ranch claims, with a young rooster named Wayne.

Cock-a-doodle-doo," Wayne was bold. "Cock-a-doodle-doo," Wayne was beautiful. But Wayne was vain and Wayne wanted fame. He teased the ranch chickens, saying they were just plain. The barnyard, he claimed, was driving him insane. For months he complained. He became quite a pain. So the chickens all told him, "then go . . . go find fame!"

So he climbed up the drain on his way to find fame. But his timing was bad. It was pouring down rain. Zap-Boom! Lightening Came! "Cock-a-doodle-Don't," exclaimed Wayne! A bolt hit the drain, killing poor Wayne. That infamous day, vain Wayne did find fame. "Wayne saved the ranch house!" folks cheered and explained. And soon they all wanted a Rooster "Weather Wayne." But the barnyard chickens knew; they saw it more plain. "Vain Wayne," they all clucked, "now weather's his fame!"

PASTA
SOUPS

Bubble, bubble,
toil it's not.
Simmer, simmer,
boiling hot.

Simple to make,
a pleasure to try,
homemade soup's
like nothing you'll buy.

Hearty Minestrone Soup

A quick, easy, and robust soup celebrating the rustic goodness of country cooking.

◆

Pick-a-Pasta: Soups are great with open shapes. We like to use heart-shaped pasta in this soup.

◆

2	cloves of garlic, minced
3	tablespoons olive oil
1	cup each chopped onion and carrot
1/2	cup chopped celery
6	cups chicken broth
8	ounces lean ham, finely chopped
1	(16-ounce) can kidney beans, drained
1	(15-ounce) can tomato sauce
1	(14-ounce) can stewed tomatoes, chopped
1	zucchini, chopped
1	teaspoon each basil and oregano
1/4	teaspoon salt
1/8	teaspoon pepper
1	cup shredded spinach or cabbage
1	cup uncooked shaped pasta
3/4	cup grated Parmesan cheese

Sauté the garlic in the olive oil in a skillet for 2 minutes. Stir in the onion, carrot and celery. Cook for 8 minutes or until the vegetables are tender, stirring frequently. Combine the onion mixture with the broth and next 9 ingredients in a stockpot. Simmer, covered, for 30 minutes, stirring occasionally. Stir in the spinach and pasta. Simmer for 12 minutes longer or until the pasta is tender, stirring occasionally. Ladle into soup bowls. Sprinkle with the Parmesan cheese.

Makes 12 servings

Approx Per Serving: Cal 203; Prot 14 g; Carbo 20 g; T Fat 7 g;
32% Calories from Fat; Chol 15 mg; Fiber 4 g; Sod 1241 mg

Super Chicken Football Soup

Prepare yourself! This chicken noodle soup will attract a crowd of football lovin' fans the size of the Super Bowl.

◆

Pick-a-Pasta: What else could you use but football-shaped pasta?

◆

4	(14-ounce) cans low-sodium chicken broth
1¹/₂	cups chopped cooked chicken
1	cup chopped carrot
1	cup chopped celery
1	cup chopped onion
2	cloves of garlic, crushed
2	bay leaves
1	teaspoon parsley flakes
¹/₂	teaspoon thyme
2	cups uncooked shaped pasta
	Salt and pepper to taste

Combine the broth, chicken, carrot, celery, onion, garlic, bay leaves, parsley flakes and thyme in a stockpot and mix well. Simmer for 15 minutes or until the vegetables are tender-crisp, stirring occasionally. Add the pasta, salt and pepper. Simmer for 7 minutes longer or until the pasta is al dente. Discard the bay leaves. Ladle into soup bowls. Add 1 teaspoon sour cream or yogurt to each soup bowl for a creamier texture.

Makes 6 servings

Approx Per Serving: Cal 260; Prot 21 g; Carbo 32 g; T Fat 5 g; 17% Calories from Fat; Chol 31 mg; Fiber 2 g; Sod 772 mg

Scrumptious Tomato and Cheese Soup

A soup for all seasons . . . . thick, creamy, plentiful, and inviting.

◆

Pick-a-Pasta: Try tree-shaped pasta in the winter or sun-shaped pasta in the sunny summertime.

◆

4	quarts water
1	teaspoon salt
1	cup uncooked shaped pasta
1/2	cup chopped onion
1 1/2	tablespoons olive oil
1	(28-ounce) can tomatoes, chopped into 1/4-inch pieces
1 1/2	cups low-sodium chicken broth
1 1/2	cups water
1/2	cup sour cream
2 1/2	cups shredded Cheddar cheese
2	teaspoons basil
	Salt and pepper to taste

Bring 4 quarts water and 1 teaspoon salt to a boil in a saucepan. Add the pasta. Bring to a boil, stirring constantly; reduce heat. Simmer for 8 to 10 minutes or until al dente; drain. Sauté the onion in the olive oil in a 3-quart saucepan until tender. Stir in the undrained tomatoes, broth and 1 1/2 cups water. Bring to a simmer. Remove from heat. Cool for 10 minutes. Whisk in 1/4 cup of the sour cream. Add the remaining sour cream and mix well. Stir in the cheese, basil, salt to taste, pepper and pasta. Cook over medium heat until heated through, stirring occasionally; do not boil. Ladle into soup bowls.

Makes 4 servings

Approx Per Serving: Cal 548; Prot 26 g; Carbo 32 g; T Fat 36 g;
58% Calories from Fat; Chol 87 mg; Fiber 4 g; Sod 1551 mg

Rustic Old-World Bisque

Continental cuisine made easy. This attractive tomato-based soup brings the best of Old-World flavor to the new world of convenience.

◆

Pick-a-Pasta: Bask in the beauty of bisque! Leaf-shaped pasta adds a flair to this European beauty.

◆

1	cup sliced celery
1	cup sliced carrot
1/2	cup chopped onion
2	tablespoons olive oil
2 to 3	cups chopped cooked pork
1	(28-ounce) can tomatoes, chopped
2	cups water
2	small zucchini, cut into 1/2-inch pieces
1	teaspoon basil
1	teaspoon thyme
1/2	teaspoon garlic salt
1/4	teaspoon pepper
1	cup uncooked shaped pasta
1/2	cup grated Parmesan cheese
	Snipped fresh parsley to taste

Sauté the celery, carrot and onion in the olive oil in a 4-quart saucepan until tender. Stir in the pork, undrained tomatoes, water, zucchini, basil, thyme, garlic salt and pepper. Bring to a boil; reduce heat. Simmer, covered, for 15 to 20 minutes, stirring occasionally. Stir in the pasta. Simmer for 10 minutes longer or until the pasta is al dente, stirring occasionally. Ladle into soup bowls. Sprinkle with the cheese and parsley.

Makes 8 servings

Approx Per Serving: Cal 274; Prot 23 g; Carbo 18 g; T Fat 12 g;
40% Calories from Fat; Chol 65 mg; Fiber 3 g; Sod 479 mg

A Home Run for Pasta

◆

Radio fans . . . This is The Big Game, brought to you by Buckeye Beans . . .

If you've just tuned in, it's the bottom of the ninth.

The score is three to three, with two outs for the Pasta Patriots; the Dullest Noodles have the field.

The Noodles have held up well so far. But now in hot water, they seem to be in no shape to compete.

With bases loaded, Pasta's best batter, Semolina Slim, takes the plate.

He's hot; spitting pesto left and right, he steps into the batters box.

The crowd is hungry . . . Here's the pitch . . . He swings. It's a Hit!

It's going, going . . . Gone! A HOME RUN!!!

Semolina Slim cooks around the bases, basking in the adoration of the Pasta fans.

Touching home, his team empties the dugout and swarms the plate . . . Slim is sauced with glory!

The crowd eats it up! Pasta fans get a big win . . . brought to you by Buckeye Beans.

From Dinner Time Stadium, this is "Whitie" Alfredo saying, "Mangia La Pasta, Baby!"

PASTA SALADS

Pasta in salad
is an American creation.
Just change the dressing
for an international sensation.

Pasta salad
is always good fun,
it's fast and easy
when you're on the run.

Sunny Mediterranean Salad

Skinny dip into the seasonings of the sunny Mediterranean with this healthy and delicious Greek pasta salad.

◆

Pick-a-Pasta: This simple pasta salad is perfect with sun-shaped pasta.

◆

12	ounces shaped pasta
1	(14-ounce) can artichoke hearts, drained
3/4	cup crumbled feta cheese
1/2	cup chopped green onions
2	tomatoes, chopped
3/4	cup vegetable oil
2	tablespoons red wine vinegar
1	tablespoon basil
2	teaspoons oregano
1 1/2	teaspoons lemon juice

Cook the pasta until al dente. Drain and rinse with cold water until cool. Combine the artichoke hearts, feta cheese, green onions and tomatoes in a bowl and mix gently. Stir in a mixture of the oil, wine vinegar, basil, oregano and lemon juice. Add the pasta and toss gently. Serve immediately.

Makes 8 servings

Approx Per Serving: Cal 422; Prot 10 g; Carbo 38 g; T Fat 26 g; 55% Calories from Fat; Chol 20 mg; Fiber 2 g; Sod 425 mg

Savory Ginger Chicken Salad

Open sesame . . . the secrets of the Orient are yours! Discover a world of rich flavor in this simple-to-make pasta salad.

◆

Pick-a-Pasta: Gingerly try baseball-shaped pasta for a grand slam salad.

◆

3	tablespoons red wine vinegar
1¹/₂	tablespoons chili sauce
1	tablespoon low-sodium soy sauce
1	tablespoon sesame oil
1	tablespoon freshly grated gingerroot
2	teaspoons teriyaki sauce
8	ounces shaped pasta, cooked, drained
2	cups chopped poached chicken
4	ounces fresh spinach, cut into strips
¹/₂	cup bean sprouts
¹/₂	cup red bell pepper strips
3	green onions, sliced
¹/₄	cup slivered almonds, toasted

Whisk the wine vinegar, chili sauce, soy sauce, sesame oil, gingerroot and teriyaki sauce in a bowl. Combine the pasta, chicken, spinach, bean sprouts, red pepper and green onions in a bowl and mix well. Add the wine vinegar mixture, tossing to coat. Chill, covered, until serving time. Sprinkle with the almonds just before serving. May omit the almonds. May substitute vegetable oil for the sesame oil.

Makes 4 servings

Approx Per Serving: Cal 453; Prot 31 g; Carbo 50 g; T Fat 14 g; 28% Calories from Fat; Chol 62 mg; Fiber 4 g; Sod 303 mg

Twist and Shout
Lime Shrimp Salad

Pucker up and bite the lime! A tangy, tart tango of shrimp, lime, and cilantro that screams with flavor.

◆

Pick-a-Pasta: With a hit like Twist and Shout, the pasta can only be stars.

◆

5	tablespoons chopped fresh cilantro
3	tablespoons fresh lime juice
1	tablespoon olive oil
1/4	teaspoon crushed red pepper
1	clove of garlic, crushed
2	cups deveined shelled cooked shrimp
3	cups uncooked shaped pasta
	Salt to taste
1	cup snow peas, trimmed
2	teaspoons sesame oil
1/2	teaspoon salt
3 to 4	green onions with tops, sliced

Combine 1 tablespoon of the cilantro, 1 tablespoon of the lime juice, olive oil, red pepper and garlic in a bowl and mix well. Add the shrimp, tossing to coat. Marinate, covered, in the refrigerator for 1 hour or longer. Bring enough water to cover the pasta to a boil in a saucepan. Stir in the pasta and salt to taste. Cook until al dente. Drain and rinse with cool water. Microwave the snow peas in a microwave-safe dish for 2 minutes. Whisk the remaining cilantro, remaining lime juice, sesame oil and 1/2 teaspoon salt in a bowl. Add the undrained shrimp, snow peas, pasta and green onions and mix well. Serve at room temperature.

Makes 4 servings

Approx Per Serving: Cal 446; Prot 28 g; Carbo 64 g; T Fat 8 g; 16% Calories from Fat; Chol 158 mg; Fiber 3 g; Sod 457 mg

Sun-Loving Salad

Sunsational! Soak up the sun in every season with this savory salad!

◆

Pick-a-Pasta: Simply accent this salad with sun-shaped pasta, heart-shaped pasta, or any other open-shaped pasta.

◆

8	ounces shaped pasta, cooked, drained
1	(6-ounce) jar marinated artichoke hearts, drained
1	(6-ounce) can sliced black olives, drained
4	ounces sharp Cheddar cheese, chopped
2	large tomatoes, chopped
1	small zucchini, chopped
1/3	cup vegetable oil
1/4	cup red wine vinegar
2	tablespoons Italian seasoning

Combine the pasta, artichokes, black olives, cheese, tomatoes and zucchini in a bowl and mix gently. Add a mixture of the oil, wine vinegar and Italian seasoning, stirring until mixed. Serve immediately. May substitute 1 cup broccoli florets for the zucchini.

Makes 6 servings

Approx Per Serving: Cal 402; Prot 11 g; Carbo 37 g; T Fat 25 g;
53% Calories from Fat; Chol 20 mg; Fiber 4 g; Sod 460 mg

... And Called It Macaroni

◆

We owe a lot to Yankee Doodle. Who outsmarted the British with a simple noodle. This song we know, from Britain it came. A Redcoat war ditty gave "Yankee" his name.

The original words made fun of our forces. Ill fed, poorly clothed and riding old horses. So the Patriots rewrote it in the American way. Using satire and wit, we returned the parley.

The new words implied, with melody snappy, "though simple and poor, we're proud and we're scrappy." When the song changed, the Brits were aghast. We rallied behind this American smash!

The tables soon turned, as the war went along. We proved ourselves able; and marched to the song. Independence was won; Yankee became fable. Macaroni's now part of the American table.

A nonsensical song; revolutionary sensation. Yankee's noodle helped make us a healthier nation.

Colorful Confetti Salad

A Yankee Doodle noodle salad that raises a flag of flavor. Light and bursting with gusto. It's an all-American favorite.

◆

Pick-a-Pasta: Red, white, and blue pasta stars, of course!

◆

3	cups uncooked shaped pasta
4	tomatoes, chopped
1/2	cup chopped green onions
1	cucumber, peeled, sliced, chopped
2	cloves of garlic, minced
2	tablespoons chopped fresh cilantro or parsley
1/2	cup vegetable oil
2	tablespoons wine vinegar
1	teaspoon salt
	Cayenne to taste

Cook the pasta until al dente. Drain and rinse. Combine the pasta, tomatoes, green onions, cucumber, garlic and cilantro in a bowl and mix gently. Add a mixture of the oil, wine vinegar, salt and cayenne and toss to coat. Chill, covered, for 1 hour or longer before serving.

Makes 8 servings

Approx Per Serving: Cal 288; Prot 6 g; Carbo 34 g; T Fat 15 g; 45% Calories from Fat; Chol 0 mg; Fiber 2 g; Sod 277 mg

The Great Grape Salad

A distinctively di'vine' pasta salad for a stomping good time.

◆

Pick-a-Pasta: A great grape salad needs grape-shaped pasta . . . or it's great with trees, too!

◆

12	ounces shaped pasta
2	cups chopped cooked chicken
8	ounces grapes, cut into halves
1	tablespoon tarragon, crushed
$^{1}/_{2}$	cup mayonnaise
$^{1}/_{2}$	cup half-and-half
	Salt and pepper to taste

Cook the pasta until al dente; drain. Rinse with cold water and drain. Combine the chicken, grapes and tarragon in a bowl and mix gently. Stir in a mixture of the mayonnaise, half-and-half, salt and pepper. Serve at room temperature.

Makes 6 servings

Approx Per Serving: Cal 486; Prot 22 g; Carbo 51 g; T Fat 22 g; 40% Calories from Fat; Chol 60 mg; Fiber 2 g; Sod 158 mg

Warm and Whimsical Vegetable Salad

*You'll go nuts for this unusual cheezie-veggie-almond blend
in a light olive oil dressing.*

◆

Rick-a-Rasta: "Habitat: Hearts Build Homes, Partnership Pasta"
is a special blend of hearts, trees, and house-shaped pasta. A portion
of the proceeds from the sale of this product goes to Habitat for
Humanity in Spokane.

◆

8	ounces shaped pasta shells
1/4	cup olive oil
2	cloves of garlic
1	teaspoon salt
4	cups cooked mixed vegetables
2	cups shredded Jarlsburg light cheese
1	cup slivered almonds, toasted, chopped

Cook the pasta until al dente; drain. Process the olive oil, garlic and
salt in a blender until smooth. Combine the pasta, olive oil mixture
and mixed vegetables in a saucepan. Cook over low heat until heated
through, stirring constantly. Remove from heat. Add the cheese and
almonds and mix well. Spoon onto a serving platter.

Makes 10 servings

Approx Per Serving: Cal 335; Prot 13 g; Carbo 29 g; T Fat 19 g;
50% Calories from Fat; Chol 20 mg; Fiber 5 g; Sod 346 mg

For Dinner That's a Hit

♦

Country, Bluegrass, Jazz or Rock

Classical, Ragtime, Rap or Pop,

Rhythm and Blues, whatever's your thing

Musical Pasta makes dinners that <u>swing!</u>

Polka, Reggae, the Latin Sound,

Metal, Folk or a musical round,

Pasta for Opera, or a slow Waltz-a

Try it with anything . . . how about Salsa?!

PASTA ENTREES & SAUTES

The day is done.
You don't want to cook.
So go boil some water
and open this book.

Why waste time stewing
over "what's for dinner?"
when these easy entrées
are simply a winner.

Perfect-Pitch Primavera

A dinner of note! A fresh, light sauté that sings of spring.

◆

Pick-a-Pasta: Perfectly tuned for musical-note-shaped pasta.

◆

3	cups shaped pasta
2	carrots, julienned
2	cloves of garlic, minced
1/2	cup chopped red onion
2	tablespoons olive oil
24	asparagus spears, cut into 1-inch pieces
20	small cherry tomatoes, cut into halves
1	red bell pepper, thinly sliced
1/2	cup low-sodium chicken broth
2	tablespoons drained capers
4	teaspoons lemon juice
1	tablespoon thyme

Cook the pasta until al dente; drain. Sauté the carrots, garlic and red onion in the olive oil in a skillet for 4 to 5 minutes or until tender. Stir in the asparagus, cherry tomatoes, red pepper, broth, capers, lemon juice and thyme. Cook until the vegetables are tender-crisp, stirring frequently. Stir in the pasta. Cook just until heated through, stirring frequently.

Makes 6 servings

Approx Per Serving: Cal 282; Prot 9 g; Carbo 49 g; T Fat 6 g;
18% Calories from Fat; Chol 0 mg; Fiber 4 g; Sod 176 mg

What to do with Zucchini!

You'll never ask again what to do with zucchini. This rich Italian-style dish is a delightful solution.

◆

Pick-a-Pasta: To know zucchini is to love zucchini, so we suggest heart-shaped pasta.

◆

³/₄	cup chopped onion
2	cloves of garlic, minced
1	tablespoon olive oil
1	cup sliced carrot rounds
8	ounces zucchini, cut into 1-inch pieces
1	(14-ounce) can artichoke hearts, cut into quarters
1	(14-ounce) can stewed tomatoes
1	teaspoon oregano
1	teaspoon basil
	Salt and pepper to taste
8	ounces shaped pasta, cooked
	Ricotta Salta to taste

Sauté the onion and garlic in the olive oil in a nonstick sauté pan for 1 minute. Add the carrots. Sauté for 5 minutes or until tender. Stir in the zucchini. Sauté for 2 minutes. Add the artichokes, undrained tomatoes, oregano, basil, salt and pepper and mix well. Simmer for 8 to 10 minutes or until of the desired consistency, stirring occasionally. Stir in the hot cooked pasta gradually. Spoon onto individual plates. Sprinkle with the Ricotta Salta. May substitute grated Romano cheese for the Ricotta Salta.

Makes 4 servings

Approx Per Serving: Cal 321; Prot 11 g; Carbo 61 g; T Fat 5 g;
13% Calories from Fat; Chol 0 mg; Fiber 5 g; Sod 589 mg

Pick-a-Peck o' Peppers and Pasta

Peter Piper never had it so good. This savory sauté rings with bell peppers in a medley of color!

◆

Pick-a-Pasta: For the fall, pick a pack of pumpkin-shaped pasta, or in the summer let sun-shaped pasta shine.

◆

3	ounces sun-dried tomatoes, sliced
1	red bell pepper, sliced
1	yellow bell pepper, sliced
1	green bell pepper, sliced
1	bunch leeks, sliced
1/4	cup olive oil
2	teaspoons garlic
2	teaspoons oregano
1	teaspoon basil
1	teaspoon thyme
1	teaspoon salt
1/4	teaspoon pepper
15	ounces shaped pasta, cooked, drained

Soak the sun-dried tomatoes using package directions; drain. Process in a blender until puréed. Sauté the bell peppers and leeks in the olive oil in a skillet until tender but firm. Add the tomatoes, garlic, oregano, basil, thyme, salt, pepper and pasta and mix well. Serve warm.

Makes 6 servings

Approx Per Serving: Cal 442; Prot 13 g; Carbo 76 g; T Fat 11 g; 22% Calories from Fat; Chol 0 mg; Fiber 6 g; Sod 675 mg

Savory Smoked Salmon Sauté

Like timpani thundering and cymbals crashing, this symphony of savory herbs, garlic, pecans, and pasta will take your senses to a crescendo of flavor.

◆

Pick-a-Pasta: Musical notes pasta is the only choice, unless of course you choose Symphony of Angels.

◆

1	cup chopped red onion
2	cloves of garlic, minced
2	tablespoons olive oil
2	cups broccoli florets
1	teaspoon thyme
1/2	teaspoon basil
1	cup chicken broth
2	tablespoons fresh lemon juice
1	cup small whole black olives
1/2	cup pecan pieces
8	ounces shaped pasta, cooked, drained
	Salt and pepper to taste
4 to 6	ounces smoked salmon, shredded

Sauté the red onion and garlic in the olive oil in a nonstick sauté pan for 2 minutes. Add the broccoli, thyme and basil. Sauté for several minutes longer. Stir in the broth and lemon juice. Cook just until the broccoli is tender-crisp, stirring constantly. Add the black olives, pecans and pasta and mix well. Season with salt and pepper. Ladle into warm serving bowls. Top each serving with the smoked salmon.

Makes 4 servings

Approx Per Serving: Cal 483; Prot 19 g; Carbo 53 g; T Fat 23 g; 41% Calories from Fat; Chol 10 mg; Fiber 5 g; Sod 682 mg

Hungarian Paprikash

You'll never be "Hungary" again with this wonderful,
savory Old-World favorite.

◆

Pick-a-Pasta: This recipe of the world deserves nothing less than
universal sportsball-shaped pasta.

◆

1   (3-pound) chicken, cut up
1   large green bell pepper, chopped
1   large onion, chopped
2   large cloves of garlic, minced
1   (28-ounce) can stewed tomatoes
4   teaspoons paprika
12 ounces shaped pasta
    Salt and pepper to taste

Rinse the chicken. Combine the chicken with enough water to cover
by 1 inch in a stockpot. Bring to a boil and stir; reduce heat. Simmer,
covered, for 45 minutes. Remove the chicken, reserving the broth.
Cool slightly. Chop the chicken, discarding the skin and bones. Stir
the green pepper, onion, garlic, undrained tomatoes and paprika into
the reserved broth. Boil over medium heat for 15 minutes or until the
vegetables are tender. Add the pasta. Cook for 10 minutes or until the
pasta is of the desired degree of doneness, stirring occasionally. May
add additional water for desired degree of consistency. Stir in the
chicken. Cook just until heated through. Season with salt and pepper.

Makes 8 servings

Approx Per Serving: Cal 360; Prot 32 g; Carbo 42 g; T Fat 7 g;
18% Calories from Fat; Chol 75 mg; Fiber 4 g; Sod 329 mg

Marvelous Marinara Hot Dish

A lusciously layered lasagna that's an easy and unusual alternative to an American favorite.

◆

Pick-a-Pasta: Like stacking firewood, try this one with pasta-shaped trees . . . if you please.

◆

15	ounces shaped pasta
1	tablespoon olive oil
15	ounces ricotta cheese
1/4	cup grated Parmesan cheese
1	egg, beaten
1/8	teaspoon nutmeg
1	(28-ounce) jar marinara sauce
1/2	cup loosely packed torn fresh basil
1	pound mozzarella cheese, shredded

Cook the pasta using package directions; drain. Combine the pasta and olive oil in a bowl and toss to coat. Combine the ricotta cheese, Parmesan cheese, egg and nutmeg in a bowl and mix well. Spread a small amount of the marinara sauce in a shallow 9x13-inch baking dish. Layer with 1/4 of the pasta and 1/4 of the remaining marinara sauce; sprinkle with some of the basil. Top with a second layer of pasta. Spread with the ricotta cheese mixture and sprinkle with some of the basil. Top with a third layer of pasta. Sprinkle with the mozzarella cheese and the remaining basil. Top with the remaining pasta; spread with the remaining marinara sauce. Bake at 350 degrees for 45 minutes. Let stand for 15 minutes before serving.

Makes 8 servings

Approx Per Serving: Cal 556; Prot 28 g; Carbo 53 g; T Fat 27 g;
43% Calories from Fat; Chol 100 mg; Fiber 1 g; Sod 948 mg

Bountiful Beef and
Ginger Stir-Fry

You can't go wrong with this quick and easy stir-fry.

◆

Pick-a-Pasta: For a true autumn experience, toss in football-shaped pasta or colorful leaf-shaped pasta.

◆

3	tablespoons vegetable oil
1	tablespoon minced fresh gingerroot
1	clove of garlic, minced
8	ounces thinly sliced beef
1	tablespoon flour
$^1/_2$	cup chicken or beef bouillon
2	tablespoons mirin
1	teaspoon red miso
1	bunch green onions, sliced
2	teaspoons water
1	teaspoon cornstarch
8	ounces shaped pasta, cooked, drained

Heat a wok over high heat. Add the oil, gingerroot and garlic. Stir-fry for 30 seconds. Add the beef and flour and mix well. Stir-fry until the beef is of the desired degree of doneness. Add the bouillon, mirin, miso and green onions and mix well. Bring to a boil. Stir in a mixture of the water and cornstarch. Cook until thickened, stirring constantly. Spoon the hot pasta onto a serving platter; top with the beef mixture. May substitute ground beef for the sliced beef.

Makes 4 servings

Approx Per Serving: Cal 456; Prot 26 g; Carbo 47 g; T Fat 17 g; 33% Calories from Fat; Chol 54 mg; Fiber 2 g; Sod 276 mg

Baseballs, Bats, and Meatballs Marinara

Step up to the plate and catch the flavor of the great American pasta-time. This healthier, slimmed-down version of classic spaghetti and meatballs is a sure winner!

◆

Pick-a-Pasta: Take me out to the ball game and toss in baseball-shaped pasta.

◆

1	pound lean ground turkey
1	onion, finely chopped
2	slices bread, crumbled
2	eggs, beaten
2	tablespoons soy sauce
1/2	teaspoon basil
1/4	teaspoon ground pepper
1/4	teaspoon garlic powder
1	(28-ounce) jar marinara sauce
15	ounces shaped pasta, cooked, drained

Combine the ground turkey, onion, bread, eggs, soy sauce, basil, pepper and garlic powder in a bowl and mix well. Shape into meatballs. Brown 1/2 of the meatballs in a nonstick skillet; drain. Repeat the process with the remaining meatballs. Combine the marinara sauce and meatballs in a saucepan. Simmer for 30 minutes, stirring occasionally. Spoon the hot pasta onto a serving platter; top with the meatballs and sauce.

Makes 6 servings

Approx Per Serving: Cal 546; Prot 30 g; Carbo 74 g; T Fat 15 g; 25% Calories from Fat; Chol 129 mg; Fiber 2 g; Sod 1309 mg

Mucho Nacho Casserole

A hot crowd-pleaser. This spicy southwestern sensation is perfect anytime and anywhere.

◆

Pick-a-Pasta: Sun worshipers of the Southwest would use sun-shaped pasta.

◆

1	pound lean ground beef
1	cup chopped onion
1	envelope taco seasoning mix
3/4	cup water
1	(4-ounce) can green chiles, drained
1/4	cup hot sauce
2	cups uncooked shaped pasta, cooked, drained
1	(10-ounce) package frozen corn, thawed, drained
1	cup sliced black olives
1 3/4	cups shredded sharp Cheddar cheese
1 3/4	cups shredded Monterey Jack cheese

Brown the ground beef with the onion in a skillet, stirring until the ground beef is crumbly; drain. Stir in the taco seasoning mix and water. Simmer for 2 minutes, stirring occasionally. Add the chiles and hot sauce and mix well. Combine the pasta, corn and black olives in a bowl and mix gently. Fold in the ground beef mixture, 2/3 of the Cheddar cheese and 2/3 of the Monterey Jack cheese. Spoon into a buttered 9x13-inch glass baking dish. Sprinkle with the remaining cheese. Bake at 350 degrees until heated through and bubbly. Cover with foil halfway through the baking process to prevent the pasta from drying out. Serve on a bed of iceberg lettuce garnished with sour cream, guacamole and tortilla chips.

Makes 8 servings

Approx Per Serving: Cal 499; Prot 30 g; Carbo 36 g; T Fat 27 g;
48% Calories from Fat; Chol 90 mg; Fiber 3 g; Sod 1062 mg

Heavenly Sauté

As delicate as a cloud. As inviting as a clear, starry night. This creamy herb and olive oil sauté is as light as an angel on wing.

◆

Pick-a-Pasta: This heavenly recipe is irresistible to pasta angels.

◆

1	pound boneless skinless chicken breasts
2	tablespoons olive oil
2	cloves of garlic, minced
1	carrot, sliced into 2-inch matchsticks
1/2	red bell pepper, cut into thin strips
2	green onions, chopped
1	teaspoon basil
1/2	teaspoon rosemary
4	ounces small pea pods
1/4	cup dry white wine
1	cup low-fat evaporated milk
8	ounces shaped pasta, cooked, drained
	Salt and pepper to taste

Rinse the chicken and pat dry; chop. Sauté the chicken in 1 tablespoon of the olive oil in a nonstick sauté pan for 5 minutes or until tender. Remove the chicken to a platter; keep warm. Heat the remaining olive oil and garlic in the sauté pan. Add the carrot, red pepper, green onions, basil and rosemary. Sauté for 5 minutes or until the carrot is tender. Stir in the pea pods and white wine. Simmer for several minutes or until most of the wine is absorbed, stirring constantly. Stir in the evaporated milk and mix well. Simmer for 5 minutes or until reduced to the desired consistency; sauce should be thin. Add the chicken and hot pasta and mix gently. Season with salt and pepper. Garnish each serving with a sprig of rosemary.

Makes 4 servings

Approx Per Serving: Cal 503; Prot 40 g; Carbo 55 g; T Fat 12 g;
22% Calories from Fat; Chol 77 mg; Fiber 3 g; Sod 148 mg

Party 'Til The Cows Come Home

◆

In a cabin at the Buckeye Ranch
the animals held a holiday dance.

All joined in to prance and play,
except the cows; they went away.

A pig overheard the cows to say,
"Too big to dance. We'll go away."

So the little pig taught the herd to move,
and in a few weeks, they got the groove.

That holiday, when the cows partook,
the animals danced 'til the cabin shook!

Twas best darned party they'd ever known,
dancin'n the night the cows stayed home.

SEASONAL CELEBRATIONS WITH PASTA

Creative meals
to celebrate the season.
Cook up some fun,
why wait for a reason!

Shaped pasta turns
on holiday lights,
to the "ohhs" and "ahhs"
of all you invite.

My-Funny-Valentine Stir-Fry

Share this stir-fry with someone you love!

◆

𝓡ick-a-𝓡asta: Need we say it . . . use only heart-shaped pasta.

◆

1	cup sliced boneless skinless chicken breasts
1/4	cup soy sauce
1	egg white, slightly beaten
1	teaspoon cornstarch
4	tablespoons vegetable oil
1	red chile, seeded, finely chopped
1	green bell pepper, thinly sliced
1	red bell pepper, thinly sliced
3	green onions, finely sliced
1	tablespoon minced gingerroot
	Sliced celery to taste
8	ounces shaped pasta, cooked, drained
1	(11-ounce) can mandarin oranges
2	tablespoons hot water
	Salt to taste

Rinse the chicken and pat dry. Combine the soy sauce, egg white and cornstarch in a bowl and mix well. Add the chicken, stirring to coat. Heat 3 tablespoons of the oil in a wok. Add the chicken mixture. Stir-fry for 2 minutes. Remove the chicken to a platter. Add the remaining 1 tablespoon oil to the wok. Stir in the red chile, green pepper, red pepper, green onions, gingerroot and celery. Stir-fry for several seconds. Add the chicken. Stir-fry for 1 minute. Stir in the pasta, mandarin oranges, hot water and salt. Stir-fry for 1 to 2 minutes or until the chicken is tender and the vegetables are tender-crisp. May substitute canned pineapple for the mandarin oranges.

Makes 4 servings

Approx Per Serving: Cal 452; Prot 21 g; Carbo 57 g; T Fat 16 g;
32% Calories from Fat; Chol 30 mg; Fiber 3 g; Sod 1078 mg

46

Lemon Asparagus Spring Sauté

There's a taste of spring in this quick-like-a-bunny, garden-light sauté.

◆

Pick-a-Pasta: The fresh vegetables in this recipe invite funny bunny-shaped pasta.

◆

3	cups uncooked shaped pasta
10 to 12	fresh asparagus spears, cut into pieces
1	cup sliced carrot
2	teaspoons olive oil
1	cup sliced fresh mushrooms
1/4	cup water
2	teaspoons minced garlic
2	teaspoons grated lemon peel
1/2	teaspoon chicken bouillon granules
1/2	teaspoon salt
1/2	teaspoon pepper
1/3	cup grated asiago cheese

Combine the pasta with enough water to cover in a saucepan. Boil for 5 minutes. Add the asparagus. Cook for 4 minutes longer or until the pasta is tender and the asparagus is tender-crisp; drain and keep warm. Sauté the carrot in the olive oil in a sauté pan for 3 minutes. Add the mushrooms. Sauté for 2 minutes longer. Stir in the water, garlic, lemon peel, bouillon granules, salt and pepper. Bring to a boil. Boil for 1 minute, stirring frequently. Add the pasta mixture and cheese and mix gently. Spoon onto a serving platter. Garnish with lemon slices.

Makes 10 servings

Approx Per Serving: Cal 148; Prot 6 g; Carbo 26 g; T Fat 2 g;
15% Calories from Fat; Chol 3 mg; Fiber 1 g; Sod 179 mg

47

South-of-the-Border Casser-Olé!

Ah, carumba some cheese on top of this big, spicy southwestern dish!
This casserole will feed a hacienda full of wild westerners!

◆

Ρick-a-Ρasta: For a casserole with this much kick, try it with
sportsball-shaped pasta.

◆

12 ounces shaped pasta
1   cup chopped onion
3/4 cup finely chopped green bell pepper
1   tablespoon minced garlic
2   tablespoons butter
1   pound lean ground beef
2   cups finely chopped mushrooms
3   tablespoons chili powder
    Salt and pepper to taste
    Cayenne to taste
2   (15-ounce) cans tomato sauce
1   (17-ounce) can cream-style corn
1   (4-ounce) can green chiles
1   (2-ounce) can black olives, drained
1   cup shredded Cheddar cheese

Cook the pasta using package directions. Rinse with cold water until
cool; drain. Sauté the onion, green pepper and garlic in the butter in a
sauté pan over medium heat until the vegetables are tender. Add the
ground beef and mushrooms. Sauté for 5 minutes or until the ground
beef is cooked through; drain. Stir in the chili powder, salt, pepper and
cayenne. Combine the pasta, ground beef mixture and next 4
ingredients in a bowl. Spoon into a greased 9x13-inch baking dish;
sprinkle with the cheese. Bake at 350 degrees for 30 minutes.

Makes 8 servings

Approx Per Serving: Cal 476; Prot 25 g; Carbo 57 g; T Fat 18 g;
33% Calories from Fat; Chol 65 mg; Fiber 6 g; Sod 1207 mg

Italian Sunsation Salad

A little taste of Italy to satisfy a big Italian taste. Perfect for a summer picnic, a light evening meal, or a romantic dinner with your favorite big Italian.

◆

Pick-a-Pasta: The essential summer ingredient is sun-shaped pasta. But for a romantic dinner, use heart-shaped pasta.

◆

1/2	cup olive oil
1/4	cup balsamic vinegar
1/4	cup grated Parmesan cheese
2	cloves of garlic, minced
1	teaspoon thyme
1	teaspoon oregano
3	cups uncooked shaped pasta, cooked, drained
1	cup cubed Italian salami
1	cup cubed mozzarella cheese
1	cup pitted medium black olives
4	green onions, sliced
4	ounces fresh mushrooms, cut into quarters
1	(4-ounce) can mild green chiles, drained, chopped
1	red bell pepper, thinly sliced
	Salt and pepper to taste

Whisk the olive oil, balsamic vinegar, Parmesan cheese, garlic, thyme and oregano in a bowl. Combine the pasta, salami, mozzarella cheese, black olives, green onions, mushrooms, chiles and red pepper in a bowl and mix well. Add the olive oil mixture and mix well. Season with salt and pepper. May substitute white wine vinegar for balsamic vinegar and green olives for the black olives.

Makes 10 servings

Approx Per Serving: Cal 300; Prot 9 g; Carbo 27 g; T Fat 17 g; 52% Calories from Fat; Chol 17 mg; Fiber 2 g; Sod 367 mg

Frighteningly Good Tuna Casserole

Warm up a bone-chilling autumn evening with this bubbling cheesy cauldron of wickedly tempting tuna.

◆

Pick-a-Pasta: Hee, hee, hee . . . Of course, we recommend jack-o'-lantern-shaped pasta.

◆

1/3	cup butter
2/3	cup flour
1	teaspoon thyme
1/2	teaspoon salt
1/8	teaspoon nutmeg
1	cup low-sodium chicken broth
1	cup milk
1/2	cup white wine
3/4	cup grated Parmesan cheese
2	(7-ounce) cans water-pack tuna, drained
1	(4-ounce) can mushrooms, drained
1	cup chopped green onions
3	cups uncooked shaped pasta, cooked, drained

Melt the butter in a large nonstick skillet. Add the flour gradually, stirring constantly. Stir in the thyme, salt and nutmeg. Add the broth, milk and white wine gradually, stirring constantly. Cook until thickened, stirring constantly. Stir in the cheese. Cook just until blended, stirring constantly. Add the tuna, mushrooms, green onions and pasta and mix well. Cook just until heated through. May substitute 12 ounces sautéed sliced fresh mushrooms for the canned mushrooms.

Makes 6 servings

Approx Per Serving: Cal 523; Prot 33 g; Carbo 55 g; T Fat 17 g; 30% Calories from Fat; Chol 63 mg; Fiber 2 g; Sod 952 mg

Holiday Magic Salad

The best pasta fruit salad ever! Beyond the known world of fruit salads, this sweet tangy treat is pure magic to the palate.

◆

Pick-a-Pasta: While any evergreen pasta tree will do, a salad this special deserves Buckeye's unique "Christmas Trees and Toys Pasta."

◆

4	quarts cold water
1	teaspoon salt
15	ounces shaped pasta
1	pound boneless skinless chicken breasts, cooked, chopped
1	cup red and green grape halves
1/2	cup chopped apple
1/2	cup sliced banana
	Sections of 3 oranges
1	bunch green onions, sliced
3/4	cup frozen orange juice concentrate, thawed
1/4	cup vegetable oil
1/4	cup white wine vinegar
1	teaspoon salt
1/2	teaspoon pepper

Bring the cold water and 1 teaspoon salt to a boil in a saucepan. Add the pasta. Bring to a boil, stirring constantly; reduce heat. Simmer for 8 to 10 minutes or until al dente; drain. Combine the pasta, chicken, grapes, apple, banana, orange sections and green onions in a bowl and mix gently. Whisk the orange juice concentrate, oil, wine vinegar, 1 teaspoon salt and pepper in a bowl. Pour over the pasta mixture and mix gently. May substitute any combination of grapes, apples and bananas.

Makes 8 servings

Approx Per Serving: Cal 447; Prot 22 g; Carbo 70 g; T Fat 10 g; 19% Calories from Fat; Chol 36 mg; Fiber 4 g; Sod 572 mg

Mousse for the Moose

◆

The wildest Christmas at the Buckeye Ranch was when a mighty messed-up moose came for dessert. It was Christmas Eve and somehow this moose had climbed up on the ranch house roof.

By Jingle," said Black Bean Bart, "he thinks he's one of Santa's reindeer and he's a-tryin' to FLY!!"

It was time for a plan! As it happened, the Christmas dinner finale was a gigantic chocolate mousse, already whipped up in the kitchen. Ranch Cooks, Black Bean Bart, and the Pinto Kid grabbed the dessert mousse, putting it out to pasture in clear sight of the roof-sittin' moose!

That sweet temptation worked like magic, for that moose FLEW right off the roof. No moose enjoyed a lickin' more, and as he got his "just desserts" a Merry Christmas was had by all!

The Christmas Moose's Mousse

What? You're kidding? Pasta dessert?

We tried some ideas, we choose not to insert.

So here's our favorite, no one will refute,

our well loved "mousse" is a sweet substitute.

◆

1/4	cup sugar
1/4	cup rum
6	ounces semisweet chocolate
3	tablespoons whipping cream
3	egg whites
1 1/2	cups whipping cream, stiffly beaten

Combine the sugar and rum in a bowl, stirring until the sugar dissolves. Heat the chocolate in a double boiler over hot water until melted. Remove from heat. Add 3 tablespoons whipping cream gradually and mix well. Stir in the rum mixture. Let stand until cool. Beat the egg whites in a mixer bowl until stiff peaks form. Fold in the chocolate mixture. Fold the chocolate mixture into the whipped cream in a bowl. Spoon into individual dessert goblets. Chill for 2 hours. May substitute a mixture of 2 tablespoons vanilla extract and 2 tablespoons water for the rum.

Makes 8 servings

Approx Per Serving: Cal 321; Prot 3 g; Carbo 21 g; T Fat 25 g;
66% Calories from Fat; Chol 69 mg; Fiber 1 g; Sod 42 mg

Leaf it Alone

◆

*C*ascades of color, gently floating to the ground. Falling, falling, falling and blowing all around . . .

*W*hile you're raking leaves in the fall, ever wonder just what those leaves are good for? Leaves are a great source of information; just look at all those 'leaflets' you get in the mail! Leaves have played a part in Art History by protecting the human form from too much 'realism' ('Fig-ure' that one out?!). And what would literature be if we couldn't 'leaf' through a book?! When life gets dull, we make it better by turning over a new 'leaf.' When we need a break, we take a 'leaf' of absence. Or when serving a big dinner, just try to make a table bigger without leaves!!

*O*K, OK, we'll 'leaf' it alone . . . But we'll 'leaf' you with this thought: leaves would be nothing without trees. Together, the leaves and trees clean up the mess we make of our air, give us piles of fall exercise, and feed the earth by making great mulch.

*T*he next time you're raking up leaves, pondering their worth, consider this . . . perhaps what this world really needs is just good, strong "leafership!"

PLAYING WITH PASTA

"Don't play with your food,"
folks used to say,
but shaped pasta's perfect
when you want to play.

For crafts, math or science,
without any sighing,
pasta shapes expand learning
without even trying.

Playing with Pasta

There is more to learn from Shaped Pasta than just how to cook and eat it. This chapter is designed to inspire you with adventurous and creative ways of learning and playing with pasta. From simple craft ideas, to place settings and storytelling, whimsical pasta invites you to "play with your food," and we don't just mean during dinner.

Pasta Necklaces

Cut two-foot lengths of colored yarn for as many necklaces as you want to make. Dip the ends of the yarn in wax (drip candle wax on ends and pinch to points), or roll small pieces of clear tape around each end and cut to a point. This keeps the ends together, as with shoelaces, and makes stringing easier. String various pasta shapes in patterns.

Tie a knot around one piece of pasta if you want it to hang down for the center of the necklace. Sun-loving pasta necklaces or heart necklaces make great Mother's Day gifts.

Picture Frames

Gold Picture Frames

Glue pasta onto a pre-cut picture frame and spray the frame with gold spray paint.

Handmade Frames

These are easy with two pieces of construction paper. Cut out an oval or unique shape on one piece of paper. Match the outer edges. Glue only at top so the picture can be inserted. Glue on shaped pasta.

Sports Fans Frames

Use sportsball pasta, such as baseballs, bats, and gloves to make a special gift frame for the team coach.

Pasta Christmas Trees

Start with a pre-formed styrofoam cone. Glue on assorted pasta shapes, such as angels, toys, and musical notes. Spray paint the entire "tree" your favorite holiday color.

Place Settings

Decorate large pieces of construction paper with glued pasta shapes around the edges for special-occasion dinners. Special kids clubs love the patriotic look of red, white, and blue stars from the All American Pasta for patriotic events.

Spread a cup or two of uncooked pasta in the middle of a table as a centerpiece decoration. Add candles or flowers. These pretty shapes make for entertaining conversation and projects while kids are waiting for dinner. They are pretty enough to adorn the finest holiday table.

Family-Friendly Pasta

Pasta is family friendly because almost everyone likes pasta. It can be cooked up fast and eaten plain, or with fancy sauces. It is family friendly because of its versatility. Part of the pot can be served with just butter and cheese for young palates, some can have exotic sauces, and leftover pasta can be easily made into pasta salad with the addition of a little bottled dressing. Anything that is fast in the kitchen is family friendly!

Special shapes can be a simple way of enhancing family events without increasing the cost. Certain shapes become traditions that can be passed on. Heart-shaped pasta always says "I love you," even when it is served as leftovers. Sunsational Pasta adds brightness to the dreariest of winter meals.

Family friendly is also about families taking the time to cook and eat together. In this hurried world we live in, when kids can put on the pot of water to start to boil before parents get home from work, help get bowls and plates ready while the pasta is cooking, and choose which shape to serve tonight—then everyone will smile and have a satisfying meal knowing they all pitched in.

Epilogue

Ode to Making
People Smile

◆

The simplest things bring smiles to the day,
a laugh, a good meal, food made the old way.

Our recipes and pastas were created for fun,
making healthy food simple, for folks on the run.

From cooking to serving, we invite you to play,
take Shaped Pasta and adapt it your way.

An accent or change can stretch recipes for miles;
the more creative the meal, the more people smile.

Write to us!

If you have a suggestion, an idea or just want to share
a smile, drop us a line or give us a call.

Buckeye Beans & Herbs, Inc.

P.O. Box 28201

Spokane, Washington 99228-8201

1-800-449-2121

Item List of Pasta Shapes

Item Code	Description
227	Christmas Tree Pasta 15 oz.
232	Heart Pasta 15 oz.
242	Bicycle Pasta 15 oz.
245	Autumn Leaf Pasta 15 oz.
246	Holiday Heart & Home 15 oz.
247	Christmas Trees & Toys 15 oz.
248	Symphony of Angels 15 oz.
249	Musical Pasta 15 oz.
252	Bunny Pasta 15 oz.
256	Dolphin Pasta 15 oz.
258	Sportsball Pasta 15 oz.
271	Football Pasta 15 oz.
275	Sunsational Pasta 15 oz.
278	Baseball Pasta 15 oz.
285	Evergreen Pasta 15 oz.
288	All American Pasta 15 oz.
586	Habitat: Hearts Build Homes, Partnership Pasta 15 oz.

To Order Call 1-800-449-2121.

Index

About the Authors

Buckeye Beans, the food company known for "making people smile," invites you to experience the whimsical world of fun and fancy shaped pasta. Pioneers in shaped pasta technology, Buckeye took a whimsical idea for pasta design and helped forge a new market in special food manufacturing. With innovation and imagination, they helped sculpt pasta into an art form, adding color and creativity to one of the world's most popular foods. Now, Buckeye presents this creative pasta cookbook featuring health-smart recipes and zesty ideas that bring a dash of whimsy to the dinner table.

Buckeye's "bean-mark" means quality food made simple, with a little something extra to "make people smile." Purveyors of Far Fetched Food Fables on pasta packages, Buckeye products promote preposterous puns, just for fun. In this cookbook, enjoy many of these unlikely fables that promise to bring a smile to even the busiest cook.

Buckeye Beans knows much about cooking with whimsy. The company was founded on a whimsical notion. You've heard of Jack and the Beanstalk? Well, unlike the story of Jack, the Buckeye Bean story is a real-life fairy tale of a ceramic artist named Jill who, with her husband Doug Smith, discovered magic in a colorful bag of bean soup mix. No, the beans didn't grow into a giant beanstalk. They sprouted as a single product, Buckeye Bean Soup, that grew into a giant in the world of special food manufacturing. Since 1983, Buckeye Beans & Herbs has been redefining convenience, by creating healthy, natural, quality products that make good-tasting food simple to make. Buckeye expanded into pasta production in the early '90s, and now weaves gold from pasta shaped like bunnies, baseballs, bicycles, and more.

Buckeye Beans & Herbs, Inc.
P.O. Box 28201
Spokane, Washington 99228-8201
Ph: 509-484-5000 Fx: 509-484-5500

Discover the great taste of Buckeye Beans. Call for our free "Buckeye Ranch" catalog. Filled with fun, flavor and fanciful products, it's the most taste-filled catalog in the Pacific Northwest.

1-800-449-2121

Making Money with Shaped Pasta

If you want to learn about fun and making money, shaped pasta has an angle for you. Seasonal, topical, inspirational, and just plain fun, these wonderful shaped pastas have contributed well over $1,000,000 to nonprofit fund-raising causes in recent years.

Many producers, including Buckeye Beans & Herbs, directly manage fund-raising programs. One national leader, Innisbrook Wraps, pioneered shaped pasta in fund raising with Buckeye's Christmas Tree Soup. The Innisbrook program has expanded to even include this Shaped Pasta cookbook as one of their fund-raising items (1-800-334-8461).

Habitat for Humanity—Spokane, sold bags of Buckeye's pasta trees, hearts, and houses, packaged with information about their "Women's House Project." This project is a dynamic model of entrepreneurial spirit and contribution that is continuing to grow.

In the process of fund raising with shaped pasta, groups can learn a great deal about marketing, economics, health, science, finance, accounting, purchasing, advertising, and even history and art. At Buckeye we have written an educational game that enhances classroom skills while administering a healthy fund-raising business. For more information, call the F.u.n.E. Business Division at Buckeye 1-800-227-1686.

Order Form

Buckeye Beans & Herbs, Inc.
P.O. Box 28201
Spokane, Washington 99228-8201

I would like to receive_____copies of the cookbook **Shaped Pasta: Cooking with Whimsy** at $13.90 per cookbook, which includes shipping and handling. Please make check or money order payable to Buckeye Beans & Herbs.

Mail to:

Name: _____

Address:_____

City:_____State:_____Zip:_____

I would like to receive a free copy of the Buckeye Ranch Catalog.

Name: _____

Address:_____

City:_____State:_____Zip:_____

Please send a free copy of the Buckeye Ranch Catalog to my friend.

Name: _____

Address:_____

City:_____State:_____Zip:_____

For more cookbooks or the Buckeye Ranch Catalog, call 1-800-449-2121.